Very often I seem to be

much more concerned with

the monsters than with

what are called beauties . . .

I don't feel at all like the

age of graces. I like girls,

but I don't feel at all like

using that feminine grace in

concepts . . . I don't think

this is an age of grace.

Beauty is to expose the

cruelty in men

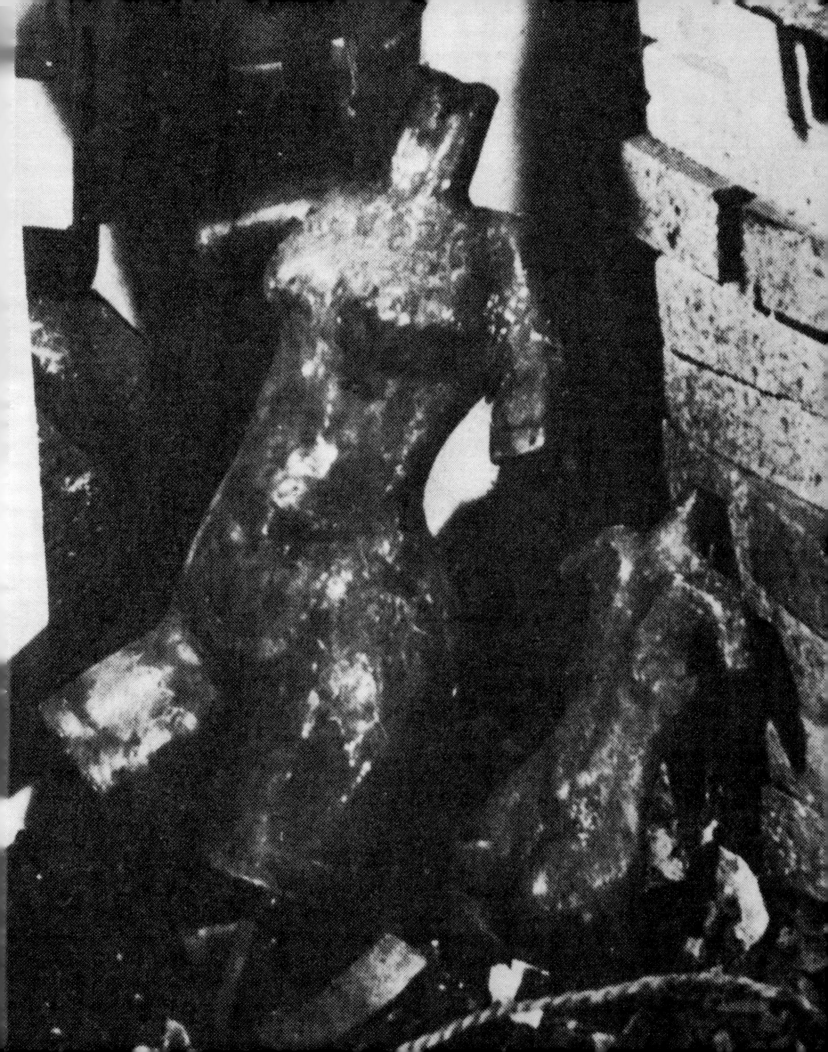

I would like to gratefully acknowledge Candida Smith, Rebecca Smith and Peter Stevens for their contribution to this exhibition and its accompanying publication. Their intimate knowledge of the work and enthusiasm for this project have been invaluable.

We especially appreciate the generous loan of David Smith's *Running Daughter* from the Whitney Museum of American Art.

We wish to thank Michael Brenson for his insightful and revealing essay.

Ann Freedman
Director
Knoedler & Company

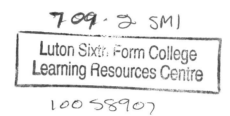
Published on the occasion of the exhibition
David Smith: To and From the Figure

Knoedler & Company
19 East 70th Street, New York, NY 10021
Telephone 212 794 0550 Fax 212 772 6932

April 29 to May 20, 1995

Exhibition travels to:

Akira Ikeda Gallery
Showa Building, 8-18 Kyobashi 2-chome, Chuo-ku, Tokyo, 104, Japan
Telephone 011 813 3567 5090 Fax 011 813 3567 5085

September 1 to September 30, 1995

First published in the United States of America in 1995 by
Rizzoli International Publications, Inc.
300 Park Avenue South
New York, NY 10010

ISBN 0-8478-1928-0
Library of Congress catalog card number 95-69010

Photo credits:
Principal photography by Deschenes Photography
David Smith Studio, page 3, by David Smith
Running Daughter, page 11, by Jerry L.Thompson,
    © 1995 Whitney Museum of American Art
David Smith, page 54, back cover, by Ugo Mulas

Opening quotation by David Smith
from *David Smith by David Smith*. New York, Chicago,
San Francisco; Holt, Rinehart & Winston, 1968. p.77

Printed by Citation Graphics, Moorestown, NJ
Designed by David Curry Design, New York, NY

DAVID SMITH

To and From the Figure

Knoedler & Company
New York

April 29 to May 20, 1995

Exhibition travels to:

Akira Ikeda Gallery
Tokyo

September 1 to September 30, 1995

RIZZOLI NEW YORK

David Smith's Embrace
By Michael Brenson

In 1964 David Smith painted a series of female nudes that he thought enough of to exhibit with his *Cubi* sculptures, which seem so different from them in their geometrical vocabulary and celebration of light and space. The paintings are, in fact, intimately related to these great sculptures, and to Smith's sculpture in general, and wonderfully revealing about Smith the artist and man. With the most direct and economical means—black or brown enamel lines running and spilling across undifferentiated grounds—Smith channeled into currents of paint some of his most basic feelings about art, nature, women and himself.

These enamel paintings are extremely personal. In his quick and candid but never entirely spontaneous responses to naked women lying and reading, standing with a foot on a stool, straddling a chair, lying spread-legged in space, or crawling like a sex slave or cleaning woman on hands and knees, Smith left himself, far more than his models, exposed. His pictorial exercises of domination and submission allowed his curiosity, generosity, sensuality, ambivalence, perversity and courage to be released. These paintings leave no doubt about his belief that artistic authenticity and growth depended upon resisting any notion of correctness and liberating himself from embarrassment and shame. Smith believed that if his art was going to make a difference it had to tell the truth of himself. It did.

That truth was astonishingly complex. Smith could be cheerful or morose, uninhibited or guilt-ridden, crude or refined, affectionate or cruel. He liked tugboat whistles and the northern lights, manual labor and classical music, the ironworks in Brooklyn and the silence of the hills. He could be outraged by the exploitation and inhumanity of the State yet willing to use almost anyone or anything in the service of his work. He was shaped by his Calvinist upbringing in the flatlands of Indiana but his esthetic was no less powerfully informed by the rolling abundance of Bolton Landing, his home in upstate New York, where, he said, "no two days or nights are the same," and nature can switch abruptly from the seductive to the severe. In Smith's work, feelings flow into all kinds of other feelings. Movement and alertness become conditions. No emotion is solitary or final.

The extensive series of nudes was made not from professional models but from photographs Smith took of the young women who either followed their daily rhythms or posed for him in his house—not in his studio—where he lived alone in the years prior to his death in 1965. All are big-breasted, full-bodied, mid-summer ripe. All are informal. Almost all are unself-conscious. Some are luxuriously at ease. A few, including the most pornographically available, reveal a capacity for venom and retribution in their predatory eyes or talon- or pincer-like feet. Most, however, are as soft and alluring yet as mutable and boundless as the earth, the kind of enveloping yet elusive creatures of nature whose presence could discharge the forces of confidence and doubt battling each other in Smith's personality and imagination.

The fact that these paintings were made with enamel is important. So is the way the enamel was applied: dripped or squeezed onto the linen or canvas with an ear syringe. The syringe, which resembles a small turkey baster, kept Smith's hand off the surface, thereby making the process of delineation looser than drawing with pencil or ink. Applying enamel with a syringe also meant the mark on the canvas was more an improvisational outburst than a stylistic signature. It meant, as well, that even while describing a body, line would not be experienced primarily in terms of its ability to describe. Enamel squeezed from a syringe hits the surface in spurts that associate the process of painting with bodily eruptions and functions. Using a syringe allowed Smith to respond to the naked female body in impulsive, unmannered ways that were not so much irresponsible as beyond responsibility.

Smith liked enamel. It had been used on canvas before him, most notably in the black paintings of Jackson Pollock, who, like Smith, came through Surrealism and believed in an essential link between technical freedom, access to the unconscious, and artistic authenticity and growth. When Smith used enamel, and he used it on some of his sculptures as well, it was still a new artistic material. It was not identified with drawing or painting from a model in the studio, or with high art, but with nail polish and car paint. Its texture has a greasiness, a vulgarity, that helped Smith tap the kind of racy vernacular urban energy he had been drawn to in himself and in America. In the late 1950's and early 60's, that energy was transforming American art.

But enamel is not anti-nature. It looks organic as well as trashy. Many of Smith's thick enamel lines have the juiciness of sprouts or shoots. Because they are glossy and fatty, each solid enamel line seems to be an artery swollen with light. As a result, the lines delineating the nudes seem not only to welcome the light of the pre-primed linen or canvas but also to suck it in. This is part of what makes the nudes seem powerful. This is what makes the relationship between figure and ground dynamic. The light and space around the lines seem to be drawn into the female bodies; when a line slackens or fades, light seems to be drained from the nude back into space. The sense of these part-real, part-fantasy nudes, and of Smith's responses to them, as fundamentally natural is built into the materials and method.

Almost everything about these nudes suggests a wildly unpredictable, decidedly non-utopian organicism very different from that of French modernist sculptors like Jean Arp and Henri Laurens, for whom nature was basically constructive and hedonistic. In Smith's paintings, growth can lead to anything. Even as it describes a part of the body—a thigh, a hip, an elbow, a hand—line can transform that limb or joint into something beyond description, occasionally making flesh ominous and Dali-like in its distended swell. With few exceptions, even the most reassuring, peaceful and lyrical nudes have the capacity to mutate into something tumescent and unknown.

When a body has the ability to change at any moment—indeed seems to be changing shape even as we look at it—that body, despite its promise of obedience and pleasure, is untrustworthy. The alluring sexuality yet uncontrollable organicism of these nudes suggests Smith's experience of a link between seductiveness and capriciousness within the female body, within nature, within the world and within him. This helps explain why, with all the uninhibited sensuality proclaimed in many of these paintings, the nudes first had to be fixed in photographs, where they could be controlled by the eye before they initiated the liquid flow of the hand.

The independence and mutability of parts is also a basic characteristic of Smith's sculpture. In the 1956-60 *Running Daughter*, the steel line rises and dips and the figure races and stops and the sculpture becomes both playful child and stately bird. Here and in the *Cubi* series on which Smith was working while he made the enamel paintings, a "normal" relationship between sculpture parts has no meaning. What begins as one thing is always in the process of turning into something else. However much the *Cubi* suggest standing or reclining figures, the relationships among the cubes, disks, rectangles and cylinders are always unexpected. Capriciousness and unpredictability are part of their sculptural identity. The irresistible, sometimes frightening, organicism in the enamel paintings is a principle of Smith's sculptural vitality and law.

No less telling is the insight the paintings' figure-ground relationship provides about the Smith sculpture in space. Surely in part because he experienced the female bodies that inspired the enamel paintings as variable, Smith remained wary enough of them, and of his own feelings, to hold himself at something of a distance from them. The desire unleashed in response to the nudes in the paintings suggests his pull toward these bodies and his desire for union with them, but because they are for him ever-shifting, always in the process of metamorphosis—always more and something other than what they seemed to be at the moment he was encountering them—Smith gives the impression that full and equal union with them was impossible.

Compare this conflict between desire and fulfillment with the magnetic relationship between the nudes and the ambient space of the linen or canvas. Space and light are drawn into the bodies. They squeeze them. They cushion them. They flow in and around them. The female body does not make them unsure. The relationship between light and space and the nudes is consummated. Space and light, not the artist, are their real lovers.

Space and light are also the sculptures' lovers. In the 1937 *Torso*, the self-assured young female nude seems more eager to have an affair with space and light than with artist or visitor. In the two torch-cut steel sculptures from 1939, both like schoolgirls striding forward, confident the world is theirs, space seems to want them as fully as they offer themselves to it. In the 1952 *Anchorhead*, Smith's first full figurative sculpture, the rings of the ballooning belly and hips of the body open themselves to space and light, which fill them, circulating in and around the curves. Space and light also flow around and through the insect-like feet and anchorhead. They know the sculpture with a voracious absoluteness of embrace of which no human being is capable.

In Smith's paintings and sculptures, space and light are almost godlike. They go where they please and take what they want, without hesitation. The burnished stainless steel surfaces, the play of concave and convex shapes, the electricity of line, make the sculptures available, welcoming space and light, sparking an intimacy between them and sculpture that many artists have reached for but few have achieved. The totality of embrace Smith desires but cannot achieve with his own body in the enamel paintings is realized in the relationship between his sculpture and nature. His sculptures are his body, his history, the female body, art history and much more. Through their metaphorical magic, they become an enduring embrace in which all that Smith felt and thought is able to dwell.

1
Dancer, 1938

2
Untitled, 1935
(#73-30.35)

3
Torso, 1937
(K #62)

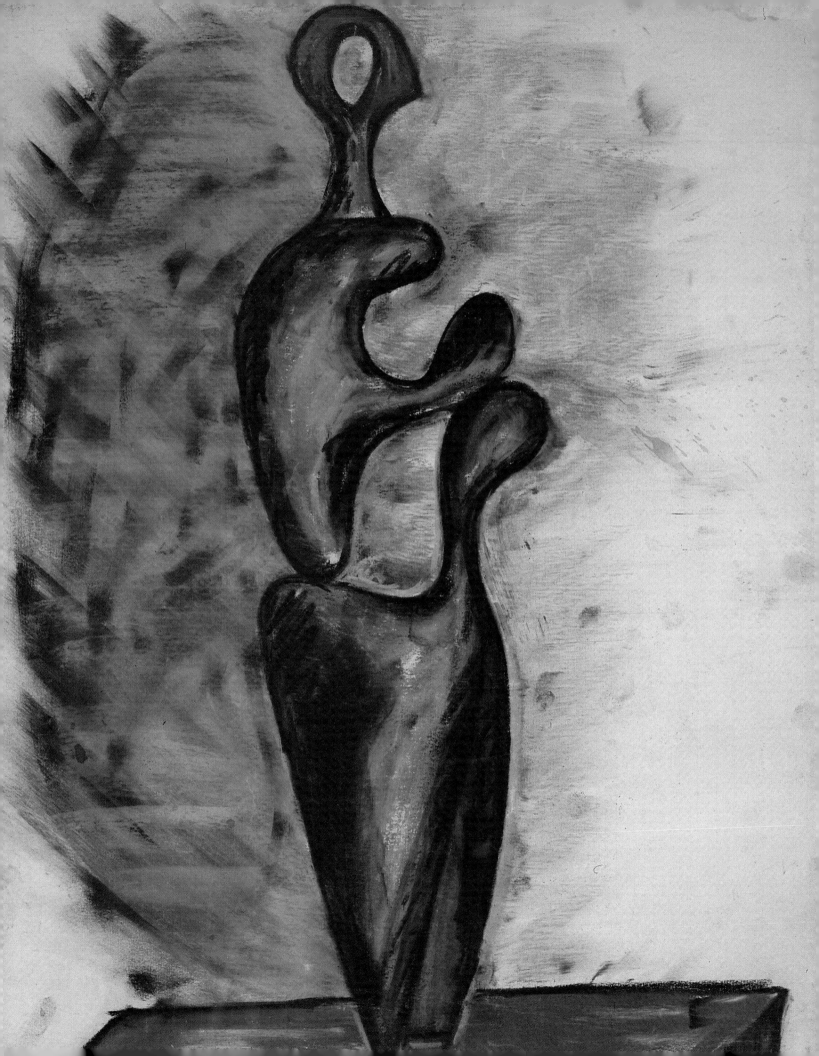

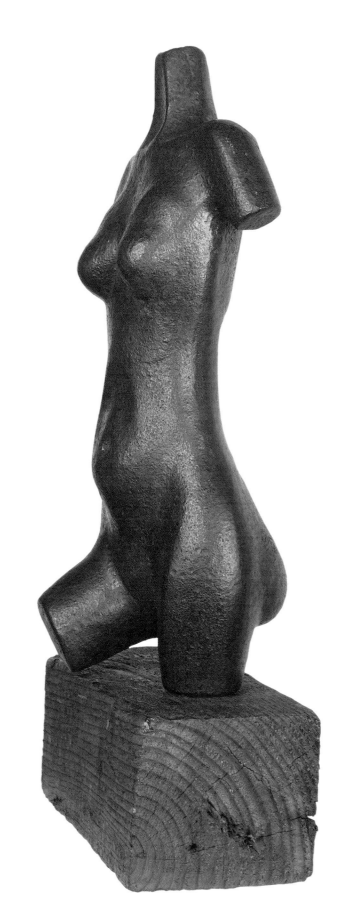

4
Untitled, 1937
(#73-37.7)

5
Torso, 1937
(K #63)

6
Untitled, 1939
(K #131)

7
Untitled, 1939

8
Untitled, 1950
(#73-50.103)

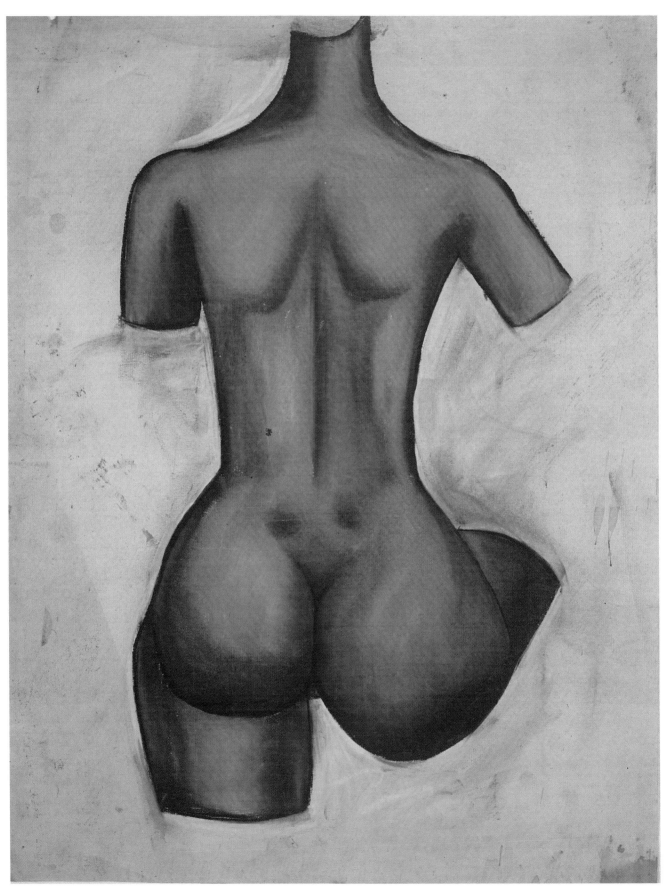

9
Untitled, (Torso Study 2), 1934
(#73-34.103)

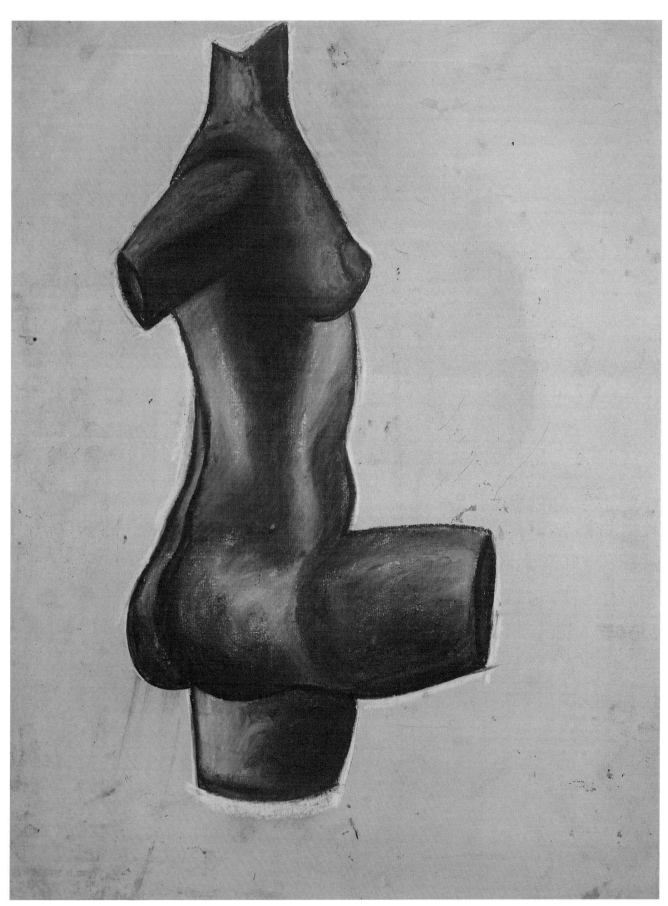

10
Untitled, (Torso Study 1), 1934
(#73-34.102)

11
Untitled, c.1936
(#75-30.143)

12
Untitled, (Torso Study 3), 1934
(#73-34.104)

13
Untitled, 1956
(K #387)

14
Untitled, 1955
(K #350)

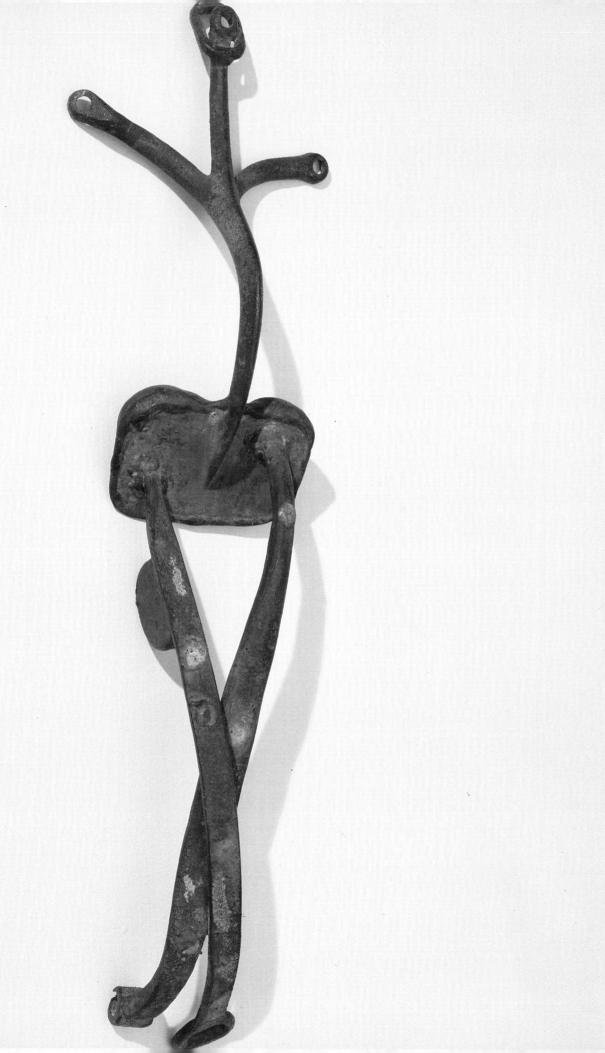

15
Figure, 1953
(K #296)

16
Untitled, 1957
(#73-57.18)

17
ΔΣ *9/5/3/53*, 1953

(#73-53.23)

18
Figure, 1953

(K #298)

19
ΔΣ *11/11/53*, 1953

(#73-53.63)

20
ΔΣ *June 1951*, 1951

(#73-51.77)

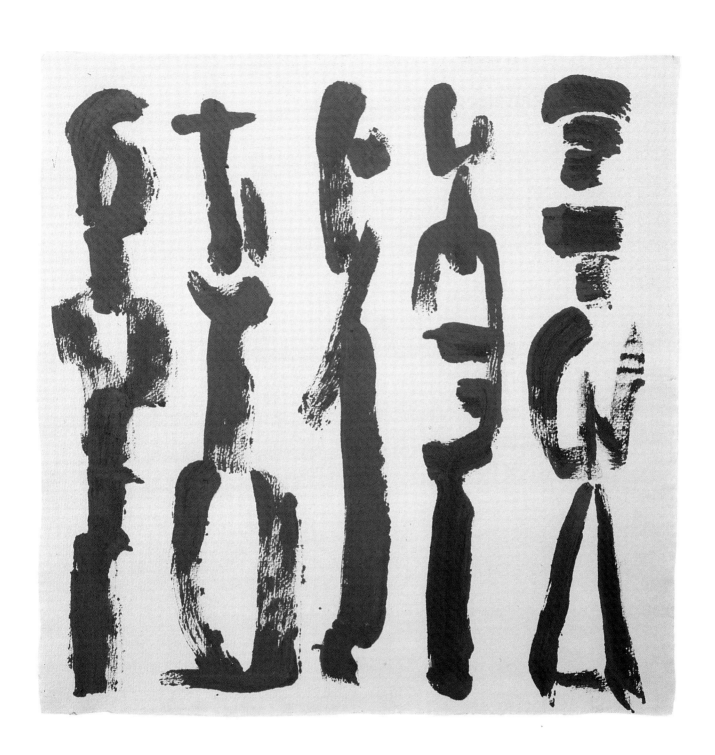

21
Untitled, 1953
(#73-53.40)

22
ΔΣ *48-12-57*, 1957

(#73-57.189)

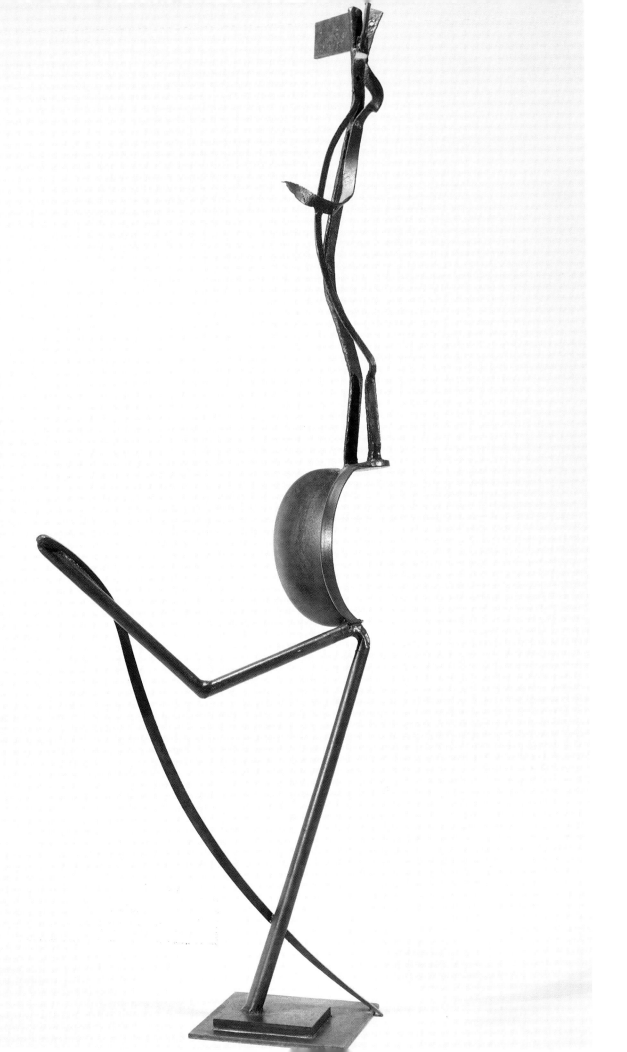

23
Running Daughter, 1956-60
(K #381)

24
28 2/54, 1954
(#73-54.125)

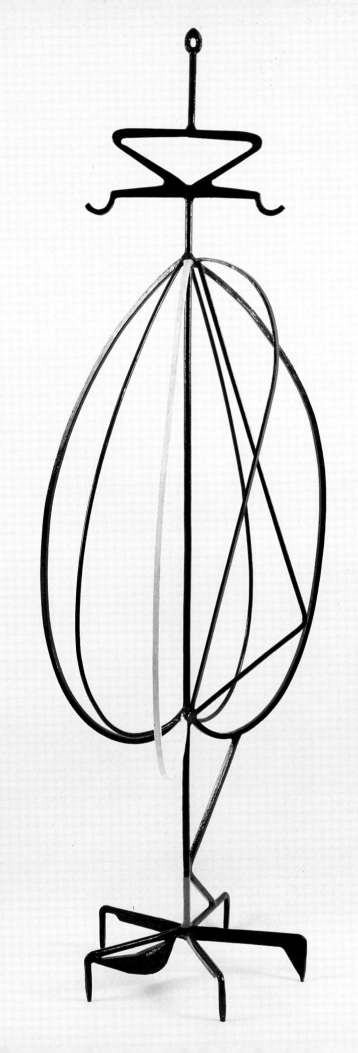

25
Anchorhead, 1952
(K #276)

26
Untitled, 1963
(#73-63.2)

27
Untitled, 1964
(#75-64.52)

28
Untitled, c.1964
(#75-64.218)

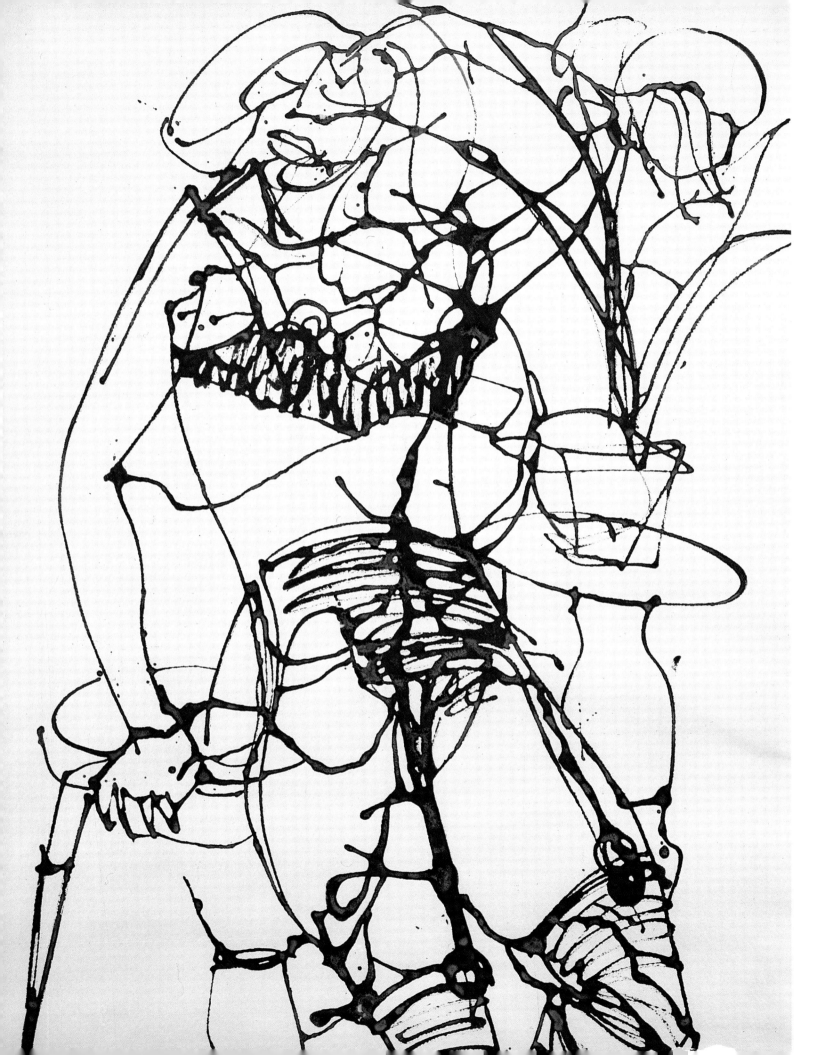

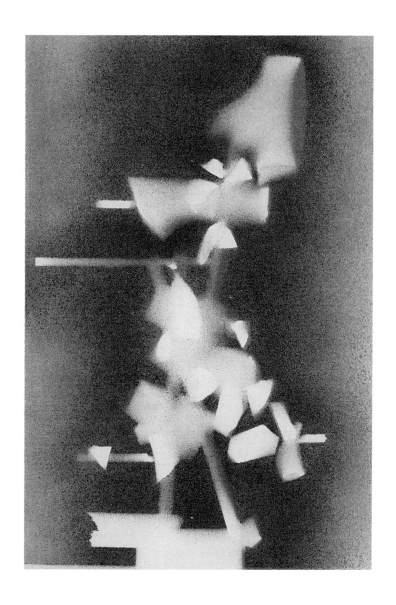

29
Untitled, 1963
(#73-63.3)

30
Untitled, 1961
(#73-61.56)

31
Untitled, 1963
(#75-63.23)

32
Untitled, 1964
(#75-64.2)

33
David Smith DO 16-1963, 1963
(#73-63.43)

34
Untitled, 1963
(#73-63.8)

35
Untitled, 1964
(#75-64.61)

36
Untitled, Study for Cubi VII, c.1964
(#75-64.224)

37
Untitled, c.1964
(#75-64.219)

38
Untitled, 1964
(#75-64.11)

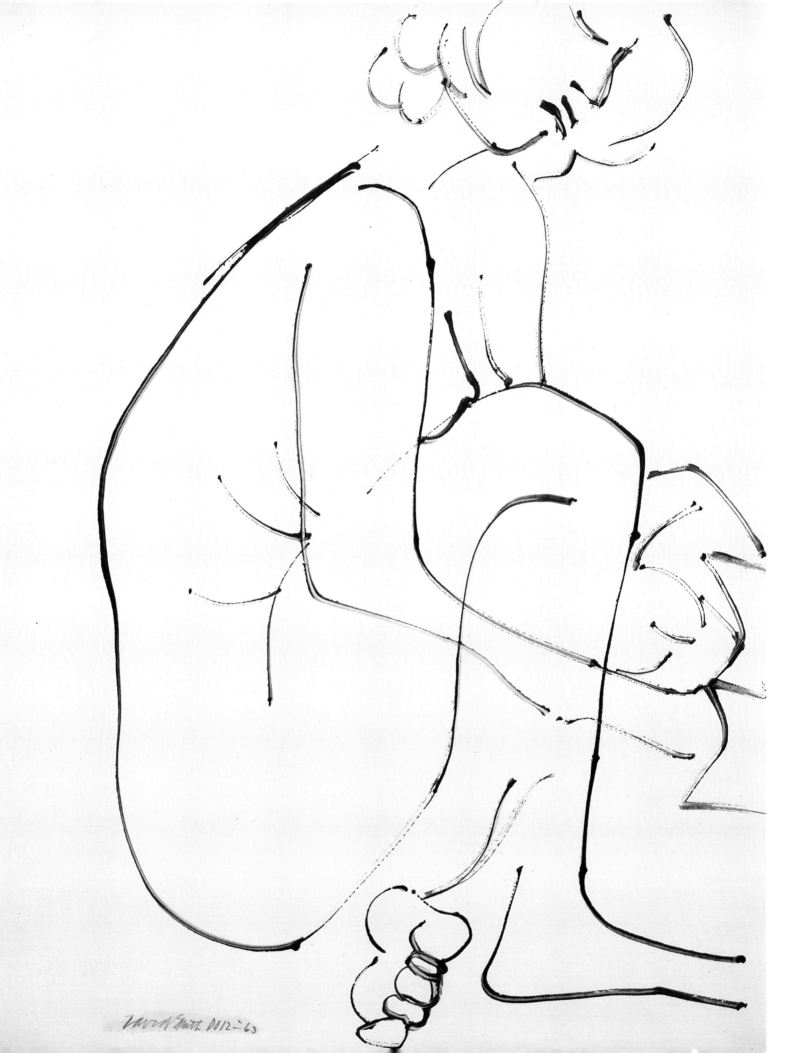

39
David Smith Do 12-63, 1963
(#73-63.39)

40
David Smith Do 17-1963, 1963
(#73-63.44)

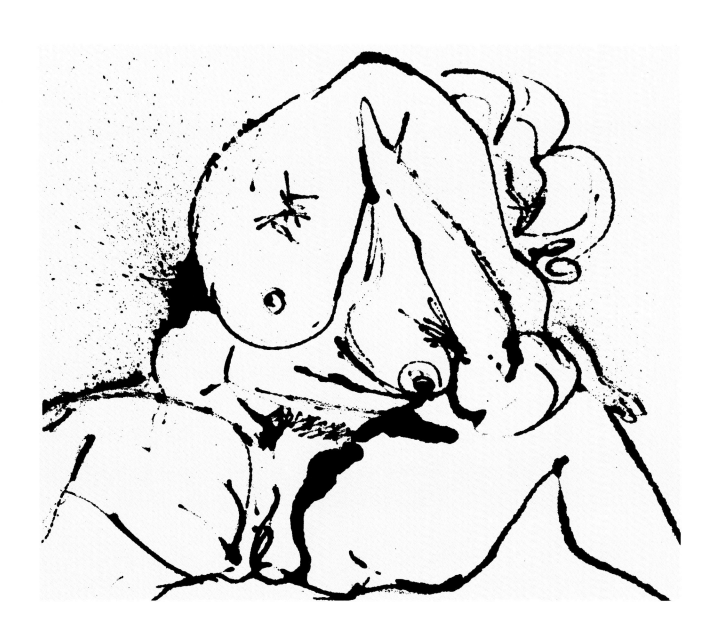

41
Untitled, 1964
(#75-64.120)

42
David Smith Mar 4 1964, 1964

(#75-64.171)

43
Untitled, 1963
(#73-63.5)

44
Untitled, 1963
(#73-63.7)

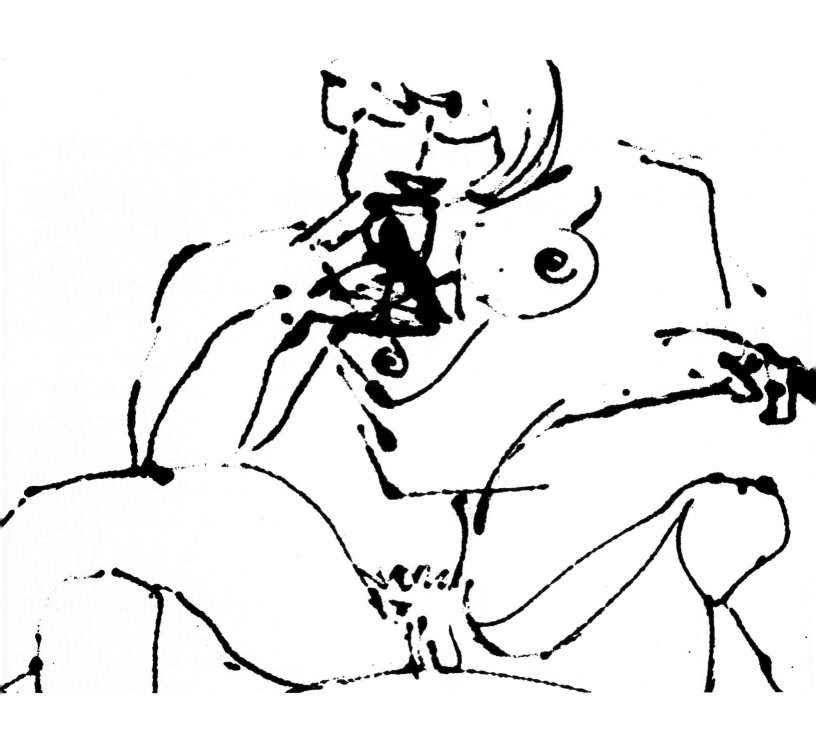

45
Untitled, 1964
(#75-64.155)

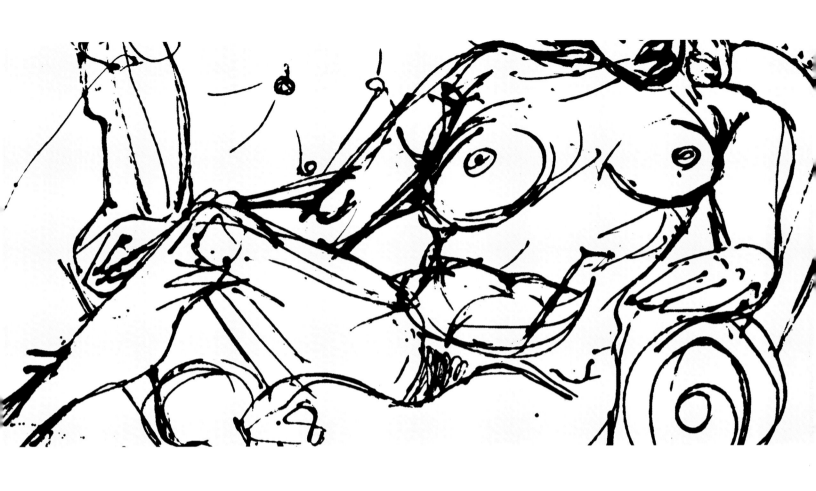

47
David S Do 1-63, 1963
(#73-63.27)

48
Untitled, 1964
(#75-64.29)

49
Untitled, 1964
(#75-64.45)

50
Untitled, 1964
(#75-64.66)

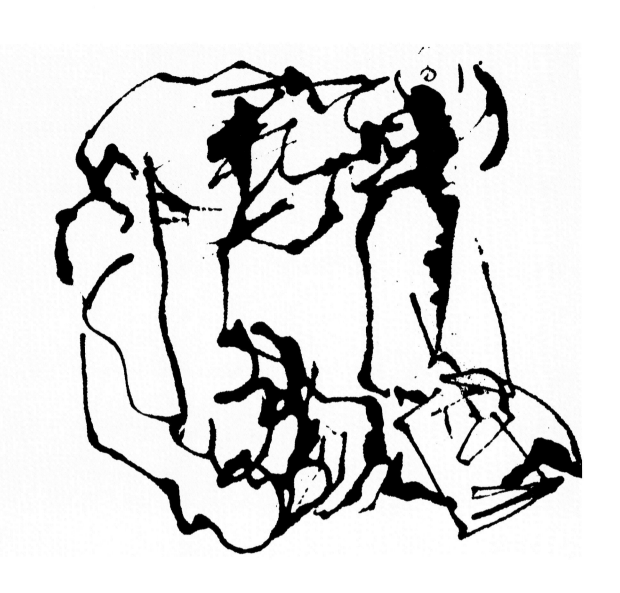

51
Untitled, 1964
(#75-64.114)

52
David S. Do 19 '63, 1963
(#73-63.46)

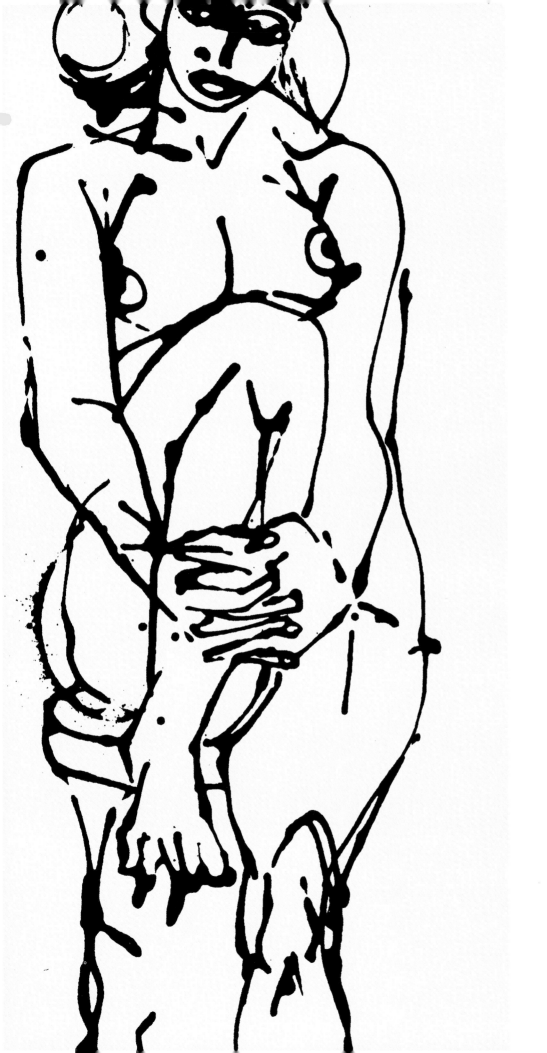

53
Untitled, 1964
(#75-64.41)

Catalogue

On Cover:
Torso, 1937
(K #62)

1
Dancer, 1938
Iron
9 3/4 x 4 x 5 1/2 inches

2
Untitled, 1935
Oil on canvas
11 3/4 x 15 3/4 inches
(#73-30.35)

3
Torso, 1937
Forged steel, painted orange
36 1/4 x 12 1/2 x 5 inches
on wooden base
25 1/4 x 13 x 13 3/4 inches
(K #62)

4
Untitled, 1937
Pastel on paper
22 x 17 inches
(#73-37.7)

5
Torso, 1937
Cast Iron
13 x 7 1/2 x 5 inches
on wood base 3 x 8 x 3 1/2 inches
(K #63)

6
Untitled, 1939
Steel
30 1/2 x 13 x 6 inches
(K #131)

7
Untitled, 1939
Steel
31 x 10 1/2 x 6 inches

8
Untitled, 1950
Ink and gouache on paper
32 1/8 x 23 inches
(#73-50.103)

9
Untitled, (Torso Study 2), 1934
Pastel on paper
22 1/8 x 17 inches
(#73-34.103)

10
Untitled, (Torso Study 1), 1934
Pastel on paper
22 1/8 x 17 inches
(#73-34.102)

11
Untitled, c.1936
Oil on canvas
15 1/8 x 11 5/8 inches
(#75-30.143)

12
Untitled, (Torso Study 3), 1934
Pastel on paper
22 1/8 x 17 inches
(#73-34.104)

13
Untitled, 1956
Steel, rusted
38 1/4 x 15 5/8 x 9 inches
(K #387)

14
Untitled, 1955
Bronze
35 7/8 x 7 5/8 x 7 5/8 inches
(K #350)

15
Figure, 1953
Steel
25 1/4 x 13 1/4 x 3 1/2 inches
(K #296)

16
Untitled, 1957
Oil on masonite
7 7/8 x 11 7/8 inches
(#73-57.18)

17
Δ Σ *9/5/3/53,* 1953
Black ink on paper
15 1/2 x 20 1/4 inches
(#73-53.23)

18
Figure, 1953
Steel and bronze
24 x 12 1/2 x 3 1/2 inches
(K #298)

19
Δ Σ *11/11/53,* 1953
Black ink on paper
7 x 10 1/2 inches
(#73-53.63)

20
Δ Σ *June 1951,* 1951
Tempera and ink on paper
19 3/4 x 26 inches
(#73-51.77)

21
Untitled, 1953
Dark green tempera on paper
12 x 12 inches
(#73-53.40)

22
Δ Σ *48-12-57,* 1957
Black egg ink on Japanese paper
17 1/2 x 22 1/2 inches
(#73-57.189)

23
Running Daughter, 1956-60
Painted steel
100 3/8 x 34 x 20 inches
(K #381)
Collection of Whitney Museum of American Art
50th Anniversary Gift of Mr. and Mrs.
Oscar Kolin 81.42
©1995: Whitney Museum of American Art

24
28 2/54, 1954
Black egg ink on paper
8 3/4 x 11 1/2 inches
(#73-54.125)

25
Anchorhead, 1952
Steel, painted black, white and
orange
76 3/4 x 25 3/4 x 21 1/2 inches
(K #276)

26
Untitled, 1963
Black enamel on canvas, Millbourn
& British handmade paper
39 1/2 x 27 inches
(#73-63.2)

27
Untitled, 1964
Black enamel on canvas
33 1/2 x 52 1/4 inches
(#75-64.52)

28
Untitled, c.1964
Spray paint on canvas
9 x 10 3/4 inches
(#75-64.218)

29
Untitled, 1963
Black drip enamel on Millbourn
paper
39 1/2 x 26 3/4 inches
(#73-63.3)

30
Untitled, 1961
Spray paint on paper
17 1/2 x 11 1/2 inches
(#73-61.56)

31
Untitled, 1963
Spray paint on canvas
19 3/8 x 27 1/4 inches
(#75-63.23)

32
Untitled, 1964
Black enamel on canvas
24 1/4 x 34 1/2 inches
(#75-64.2)

33
David Smith DO 16-1963, 1963
Black egg ink on Japanese paper
17 1/2 x 22 1/2 inches
(#73-63.43)

34
Untitled, 1963
Black drip enamel on paper
22 1/2 x 17 3/4 inches
(#73-63.8)

35
Untitled, 1964
Black enamel on canvas
50 x 28 7/8 inches
(#75-64.61)

36
Untitled, c.1964
Spray paint on canvas
14 3/8 x 15 1/2 inches
(#75-64.224)

37
Untitled, c.1964
Spray paint on canvas
9 5/8 x 12 inches
(#75-64.219)

38
Untitled, 1964
Black enamel on canvas
23 3/4 x 34 1/2 inches
(#75-64.11)

39
David Smith Do 12-63, 1963
Ink on paper
22 1/2 x 17 1/2 inches
(#73-63.39)

40
David Smith Do 17-1963, 1963
Black egg ink on Japanese paper
17 1/2 x 22 1/2 inches
(#73-63.44)

41
Untitled, 1964
Black enamel on canvas
27 1/2 x 33 5/8 inches
(#75-64.120)

42
David Smith Mar 4 1964, 1964
Black enamel on canvas
34 1/4 x 35 1/2 inches
(#75-64.171)

43
Untitled, 1963
Black drip enamel on Millbourn
paper
39 1/2 x 26 3/4 inches
(#73-63.5)

44
Untitled, 1963
Black drip enamel on Millbourn
paper
39 1/2 x 26 3/4 inches
(#73-63.7)

45
Untitled, 1964
Black enamel on canvas
24 x 30 1/2 inches
(#75-64.155)

46
Untitled, 1963
Spray paint on canvas
24 3/4 x 24 inches
(#75-63.20)

47
David S Do 1-63, 1963
Black egg ink on Fabriano paper
25 3/4 x 20 inches
(#73-63.27)

48
Untitled, 1964
Black enamel on canvas
23 3/4 x 48 1/4 inches
(#75-64.29)

49
Untitled, 1964
Black enamel on canvas
51 x 28 1/2 inches
(#75-64.45)

50
Untitled, 1964
Black enamel on canvas
51 3/8 x 23 1/2 inches
(#75-64.66)

51
Untitled, 1964
Black enamel on canvas
27 x 35 inches
(#75-64.114)

52
David S. Do 19 '63, 1963
Black egg ink on Japanese paper
22 1/2 x 17 1/2 inches
(#73-63.46)

53
Untitled, 1964
Black enamel on canvas
50 1/2 x 25 3/4 inches
(#75-64.41)